Louis Braille

Stephen Keeler

Illustrated by Richard Hook

The Bookwright Press
New York · 1986

Great Lives

William Shakespeare
Queen Elizabeth II
Anne Frank
Martin Luther King, Jr.
Helen Keller
Ferdinand Magellan
Mother Teresa
Louis Braille
John Lennon
John F. Kennedy
Florence Nightingale
Elvis Presley

First published in the
United States in 1986 by
The Bookwright Press
387 Park Avenue South
New York, NY 10016

First published in 1986 by
Wayland (Publishers) Limited
61 Western Road, Hove
East Sussex BN3 1JD, England

ISBN 0–531–18071–9
Library of Congress Catalog Card Number: 85–73675

Phototypeset by Kalligraphics Ltd, Redhill, Surrey
Printed in Italy by G. Canale & C.S.p.A., Turin

Contents

The curtain lifts

Braille is the name of a system of embossed (raised) dots, which are arranged in a particular way on sheets of paper. It is a system that makes it possible for blind people to read and write.

Reading and writing methods for the blind were clumsy and difficult until Louis Braille, in the 1840s, produced a simple system based on the domino.

Today the word "Braille" is known around the world. But in the early nineteenth century, it was just an ordinary surname.

Louis' family

On January 4, 1809, Monique Baron-Braille gave birth to her fourth child. Three days later he was baptized and named Louis.

Fifteen years earlier, Louis' grandfather, a master saddler and harnessmaker, had settled with his wife in the small town of Coupvray, a few miles southeast of Paris. By 1782, when Louis' father, Simon-René, took over the business, the Brailles had established a reputation for excellent craftsmanship.

The family was not rich. Their stone house, with its huge, moss-covered roof, was dark and gloomy inside. The windows were small and unglazed, so the heavy oak shutters were kept closed except in very hot weather. There was no running water and lighting was by candles. Their furniture was simple and practical.

But the house was surrounded by cornfields and vineyards. The Brailles kept chickens and a cow and they lived well on wholesome country food.

Like most people at that time, the Brailles had no need for reading or writing.

A historic accident

Louis Braille was a bright, blue-eyed child with blond curls. He was the baby of the family and his brother and sisters loved to play with him. As soon as Louis could talk he began asking questions and by the age of three he was taking part in the daily routine of the family.

Louis' father was very proud of his youngest son and had great plans for him. He would go to school, learn to read and write and perhaps one day enter the university in Paris and become a doctor, an engineer or a scientist.

As Louis' father worked in his saddlemaker's workshop, he enjoyed his little son's company, and would give him scraps of leather to play with. Louis would sit on the bench, watching his father working with his razor-sharp knives.

In spite of his father's warning that "Louis must never touch Papa's knives," one day, while Simon-René was in the yard, fitting a new harness to a customer's horse, Louis found himself alone in the workshop. He knew which tools were for punching, which for stitching and which for cutting, and picking up one of the sharpest knives, he started to copy what he'd seen his

Louis' grandfather founded a saddle and harness-making business which his son later took over.

father do so easily. The leather was too tough for the child and the knife slipped, the blade slicing through his left eye.

As little Louis screamed in agony, his family tried to soothe him and stop the bleeding. There were no antiseptic ointments or antibiotics in those days. The nearest doctor was more than 32 kilometers (20 miles) away, and in any case, Simon-René was suspicious and afraid of medical men. Instead, a local woman, skilled with herbal medicines, bathed the damaged eye until the bleeding stopped.

But the real damage had already been done. The eye was badly infected and soon became useless. The infection spread to Louis' undamaged right eye and within two years the child was completely blind.

The war years

Louis Braille's world changed completely. The five-year-old child had to learn his way around the house by touch and sound. He was soon back in the workshop, but would never again be able to watch his father at work. His sister, Monique, used to entertain him by telling him stories. But everything was about to change in Louis' life again.

First, Monique married and went to live with her husband in another part of Coupvray – too far from the family home for Louis to find his own way there.

Then there was bad news for the whole of France. The French emperor, Napoleon, was fighting a war in Bavaria and Russia, but in the winter of 1812 his armies had to retreat. The towns and villages around Paris had to provide food and equipment for the battered returning French army.

The village of Coupvray supplied many tons of oats and thousands of bales of hay for Napoleon's army, and cows and horses were also taken. But soon Russian armies invaded France, and on April 14, 1814, troops occupied Coupvray and seized most of the remaining food, goods and money. Almost every family in the village, including the Brailles, had to house and feed Russian soldiers.

Louis couldn't see these unknown and unwelcome visitors, who spoke a different language. And to them the child was just a blind idiot. They didn't care about him or help him the way the people of Coupvray did. Louis was constantly pushed aside or ignored. He had by now lost all his visual memory. He was confused, lonely and unhappy. He became silent and solemn and withdrew into his lonely world of private darkness.

Napoleon's army retreats from Moscow.

At school

The future was not promising. As an adult, Louis would have been lucky to make a living as a street beggar. Now, certainly, he would never be a doctor, an engineer or a scientist. But to keep his active mind occupied, his father made small leather figures for Louis to distinguish by touch, and there is a story that he made a name-board by hammering nails, in the shapes of the letters of Louis' name, into a piece of wood, for Louis to feel with his fingertips.

In 1815, a new priest, Jacques Palluy, moved to Coupvray. He heard about Louis and visited the Brailles to see whether he could help. Although Louis was still reluctant to talk with strangers, Father Palluy could see that the boy was intelligent and he offered to teach him.

At first Father Palluy came to the Brailles' house, but soon Louis had memorized the route from his home to the church, in his eagerness to spend more time with the priest. Using a simple cane his father had whittled out of a twig, the boy tapped his way up the cobbled streets of Coupvray.

Louis was a quick learner. He had no difficulty distinguishing between different birds by their song. He remembered every detail of the Bible stories which the priest told him, and he loved to listen to music.

The following year, a schoolmaster, Antoine Becheret, opened a school in Coupvray and Father Palluy arranged for Louis

to become a pupil there with the other children of the town. Sending a blind child to a normal school was unheard of in those days, but Becheret was a kind young man and the other pupils at the school all knew and liked Louis. Of course, Louis had to rely entirely on listening to the others but he developed a marvelous memory and was usually at the top of his class by the end of each term.

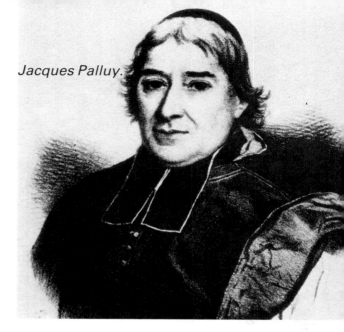

Jacques Palluy.

Being blind in the nineteenth century

Life for the blind is never easy, but in Louis Braille's time it was especially miserable. There were no trained teachers for the blind so they couldn't go to school. There was no way to teach them to read or write, and there were no jobs for them.

Blind people were often mocked and teased in the streets. They were thought of as stupid and treated as outcasts.

Louis was very lucky to have Jacques Palluy and Antoine Becheret as his teachers and also as his friends. Their kindness and concern helped him to begin the work that would eventually change for ever, not only life for the blind, but also people's attitudes toward blindness all around the world.

Off to Paris

At the school in Coupvray, Louis Braille had already demonstrated his remarkable memory and his tremendous powers of concentration. He had excellent general knowledge and had learned to discuss and work out problems. He liked to listen to Bible stories and had become deeply religious.

Toward the end of 1818, Jacques Palluy and Antoine Becheret suggested to Louis' father that the boy should be sent to the only school for the blind in the whole of France. This was the National Institute for Blind Youth, in Paris. There, they thought, he would be given the kind of help and encouragement that they were unable to give him in Coupvray.

So, early on a bright and frosty morning in February, 1819, Louis Braille, who was just ten years old, set off with his father by stagecoach for Paris.

The National Institute for Blind Youth

The Institute had been founded in 1784 by Valentin Haüy, who had also invented a system of raised wooden letters to help the blind read and write.

When Louis first arrived at the Institute he was very homesick. He had never been away from Coupvray or his family before. He enjoyed wearing the uniform of grey trousers, cashmere vest and dark blue jacket with light blue collar, cuffs and brass buttons, but the stone floors and walls of the cold, damp building had a chilling echo. However, he soon made friends, and Gabriel Gauthier, who had the next bunk in the dormitory, became his best friend.

Louis was an intelligent boy and he realized that the world of learning, which was open to sighted people, would remain

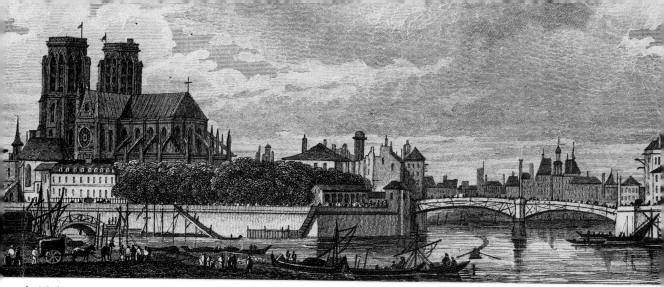

A 19th-century view of Paris showing Notre Dame Cathedral and the Seine River.

forever closed to him so long as he was unable to read or write. He was disappointed to find that there were very few books at the Institute, and that these were almost unusable because they were printed in Haüy's system of large embossed letters. Reading like this— feeling each letter individually – took a long time, and pupils had usually forgotten the beginning of a sentence before they reached its end.

So, even at the National Institute for Blind Youth, most of the teaching was carried out orally. Louis was an outstanding pupil and learned mathematics, grammar and composition with ease. He also learned to play several musical instruments by ear. He won many prizes for his work and was even made foreman of the workshop, where the pupils at the Institute made slippers. He grew to enjoy living at the Institute, although he could never quite rid his bones of the cold dampness of the place.

Valentin Haüy.

Reading and writing systems

Braille is not the only reading and writing system for the blind, and it certainly wasn't the first. Six hundred years ago, a blind professor in Persia invented a system to help him read books and make notes from them.

In the two hundred years before Louis Braille was born, many systems were developed, using carved wooden letters or wax-coated sheets into which words were cut with a stylus. One system, developed in Scotland, used string! Different types of knots, representing letters of the alphabet, were tied in the string at regular intervals. Readers

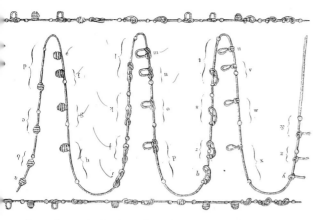

A string alphabet for the blind.

simply pulled the string from a reel and "read" the knot. They could also "write" by tying knots in the string.

In 1819, Charles Barbier, a French army officer, invented a system using dots and dashes punched into paper tape. He had developed his invention, called "Night Writing" to help his soldiers communicate with each other silently on the battlefield at night. In 1821, Barbier was invited to the National Institute for Blind Youth to demonstrate "Night Writing."

Although it was complicated, pupils at the Institute found they could read Barbier's system much more quickly than Haüy's embossed books. By using a stylus and a small metal frame, to position the dots and dashes

correctly, they could also write quite easily.

One of the pupils present at Barbier's demonstration was the twelve-year-old Louis Braille. He realized immediately that "Night Writing" offered the chance he had been looking for – the opportunity to open up to blind people the world of literature and knowledge.

"Night Writing," in its original form, was not the perfect system. It was complicated and difficult to distinguish the dots and dashes accurately with the fingertips. From now on, Louis Braille was to spend every spare minute trying to improve Barbier's system.

A battlefield at night. Barbier's "Night Writing" helped soldiers to communicate silently with each other.

From punched holes to raised dots

Louis Braille's great advantage was his blindness. He understood the problems of the blind from the inside. He knew what blind people could do and what was too difficult for them.

"Night Writing" used as many as fourteen dots and dashes for each letter or sound. This was too many to feel with the fingertips at one time.

Braille knew from his own experience that dots were easier to feel than dashes. So he got rid of the dashes and produced a remarkably simple system of dots based on the domino, using only six dots.

He also knew from experience that embossed letters were easier for blind people to feel than punched holes. He therefore took the best ideas from several systems. But the real genius was in the six dot combinations.

Braille arranged his dots in two columns, numbered like this:

1 . . 4
2 . . 5
3 . . 6

He divided the alphabet into three groups. Group 1, the first ten letters (A-J) uses only the top four dots (1,2,4 and 5).

Group 2, the second ten letters (K-T) is the same as Group 1 except that dot 3 is added each

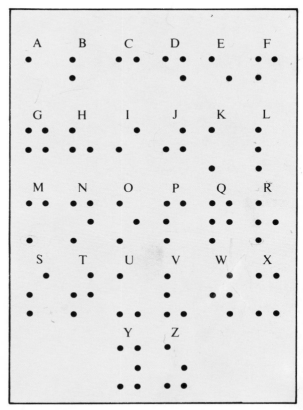

The Braille alphabet.

time (so A becomes K with the addition of dot 3).

The third group finishes the alphabet and includes some simple words. This group just adds dot 6.

W is not used in the French alphabet, but it was added to Braille later. It is made up from dots, 2, 4, 5 and 6.

Left Braille's system enabled blind people to read quickly and easily.

Opposition

A blind retired soldier slowly reads a book, using Haüy's system of raised wooden letters, which were awkward and difficult to remember.

Although Braille's system was brilliant, and although it was supported by all the pupils and many of the teachers at the National Institute for Blind Youth, it was disliked by the Institute's governors. They supported other systems of reading and writing, such as Haüy's raised wooden letters, which they knew how to read themselves but which was far too cumbersome to be efficient when used by the blind.

Because the governors of the Institute were not blind themselves, they couldn't understand the tremendous advantages of Braille. They did not realize its simplicity and the fact that it allowed blind people to write as well as to read. They distrusted a new system that they were unable to use without first having to learn Braille's language of dots. They weren't prepared to study and learn this new language.

Some of the governors also believed that since Braille was the invention of one of the Institute's own pupils, and not of some great inventor, it couldn't possibly be very good!

And so the governors of the National Institute banned the use of Braille for their pupils. Later, in 1840, they fired the principal, Dr. Pignier, when they discovered that he had had several textbooks produced in the new "dot" system.

Louis Braille must have been

very disappointed to know that all his long hours of effort to perfect his brilliant new system of reading and writing appeared to be wasted and that Braille was being ignored.

For many more years, pupils at the National Institute for Blind Youth would learn their lessons through the old accepted system of embossed lettering, which was so awkward and hard to learn.

The governors of the National Institute for Blind Youth distrusted Braille's method and forbade its use in the school.

Braille the teacher

When it came time for Louis Braille to think about leaving the Institute to seek work, Dr. Pignier, the principal at the time, offered him a job as a teacher. And so Louis Braille became a junior teaching assistant at the Paris Institute where he had been for so long a pupil himself.

Braille had always been an excellent pupil and now he was to show that he was also a very good teacher. He taught history, geography, mathematics, grammar and music, using the Haüy method of reading and writing, with raised wooden letters of the alphabet. Sometimes he and his pupils would secretly use his new six-dot system. The way he taught his pupils was very different from the way that was usual at the time. In most schools, including the Institute, teachers were very strict. They used to beat the boys regularly, believing that this treatment was the only way to get their pupils to learn.

Louis Braille, perhaps remembering his own gentle teachers, Jacques Palluy and Antoine Becheret in Coupvray, knew that students respond to kindness and patience and that they learn much more easily when their teachers do not beat them. He prepared his lessons carefully and was always patient, gentle and thorough in his teaching.

Louis had always worked hard, ever since he came to the Institute as a young boy. While he was perfecting his reading and writing "dot" system he had often worked very late into the night. Now, as a teacher, he worked

The National Institute for Blind Youth.

harder than ever and was often tired. It was at this time, in 1835, that he first became ill with tuberculosis.

A man of music

Louis Braille had always loved music. In his early years as a pupil at the Institute, he had learned to play several instruments by ear.

Not satisfied with being able to play musical instruments by ear, Louis wanted to be able to read music. So he began to adapt his six-dot system to music as well as reading and writing.

It took him many years to learn to read and write music. He bought himself a piano out of the small wage he received as a teacher. Dr. Pignier asked some of the best music teachers in Paris to come to the Institute to instruct him, and Louis became an excellent pianist.

Louis had always been deeply religious. Now that he had become an accomplished pianist, he decided it was time he learned to play "God's music" on the church organ.

Dr. Pignier was convinced that the church organ with its massive foot pedals, double keyboard and rows of stops, would be beyond the abilities of even Louis Braille. But, as always, Louis was determined to master the instrument. He talked to music teachers about his ambitions at every opportunity, and eventually he persuaded them to make arrangements for him to learn. Soon Louis was playing the organ every Sunday in a small church near the Institute, and sometimes he played at three different churches on the same day.

The Church of St. Nicholas where Louis sometimes played the organ.

The final years

Louis Braille had spent most of his life within the cold, damp, stone walls of the National Institute for Blind Youth. He worked very hard for many years, on his six-dot system and struggled to get it recognized and used officially. As a teacher he spent hours preparing his lessons and, in what little free time he

This man is using Braille's new system to read aloud to fascinated onlookers.

had, he was usually to be found in some cold and drafty church, practicing on the organ.

At the age of twenty-six he became ill and gradually he grew weaker. Sometimes he would have to stop teaching in the middle of a lesson because he was completely out of breath.

At that time there was no cure for Louis Braille's illness – tuberculosis. Despite frequent visits to his family home in Coupvray for rest and country air, Louis knew that he was dying.

In 1851, when Louis was very seriously ill, a group of his friends signed a petition and presented it to the French Government. The petition asked for official recognition of Braille as a system of reading and writing for blind people. The petition also requested that Louis Braille should be awarded the Legion of Honor, (the highest award for merit in France) for his services to the blind.

But the French Government ignored the petition and on January 6, 1852, just two days

after his forty-third birthday, Louis Braille died.

Sad to say, Braille died unknown, except for the small group of family and friends who had loved him and who were deeply grateful for his lifelong commitment to the blind. Only later did he become famous as the man who invented a brilliantly simple system of reading and writing for the blind, universally used and recognized around the world.

Postscript

In June, 1852, six months after Louis Braille's death, Braille became the official reading and writing system at the National Institute for Blind Youth in Paris. Eight years later, in the United States, teachers of the blind in St. Louis, Missouri tested all the systems they could find. In 1860, they came to the conclusion that Braille was by far the best. Although other parts of the United States continued to use different systems of teaching the blind, the use of Braille was beginning to spread.

During the following eight years, Dr. Thomas Armitage, a blind doctor in England, began studying the various systems being used in the United States

Children learning to "write" in the Braille alphabet.

and Europe. He too, decided that Braille was the best, and he set up the English Braille Printing and Publishing House in London in 1868. This organization later became the Royal National Institute for the Blind. Today the RNIB prints over 600,000 books, newspapers and magazines in Braille every year.

Since 1852, the year of Louis Braille's death, his system has been adopted by countries all over the world. Braille was introduced into Austria and also into the Soviet Union, Egypt and

Young Helen Keller using Braille to study for her Harvard degree. With the help of Braille's system she overcame the handicap of total blindness and deafness.

The dome of the Panthéon rises above the Seine River in Paris: the building is the last resting place for France's heroes.

China, which meant adapting the six-dot system into different alphabets.

Finally, on June 20, 1952, just over a century after Louis Braille was quietly buried in the graveyard at Coupvray, his body was taken to be placed alongside the greatest heroes of France, in the famous Panthéon in Paris.

Nowadays, Braille's method is the standard system for teaching the blind to read and write all over the world.

Because of the tireless work of a young blind teacher who determined to open the doors of learning for fellow blind people, millions are now able to read and write, and contribute to knowledge along with their sighted colleagues.

Important dates

1784   Valentin Haüy founds the first-ever school for the blind, in Paris.

1809   Birth of Louis Braille at Coupvray, in France (January 4).

1812   He loses the sight of his left eye in an accident.

1814   He becomes completely blind. Russian troops occupy Coupvray after Napoleon's retreat from Russia.

1815   Jacques Palluy comes to Coupvray as the new village priest. He begins teaching Louis.

1816   Antoine Becheret opens a school in Coupvray and Louis becomes a pupil.

1819   Louis goes to the National Institute for Blind Youth in Paris, as a pupil.

1821   Captain Barbier demonstrates "Night Writing" at the National Institute for Blind Youth.

1824   Braille's first system of dots is completed.

1828   He becomes an apprentice teacher at the National Institute for Blind Youth.

1834   He completes the system we know today as Braille. The system is not accepted by the governors of the Institute.

1835   Braille becomes ill with tuberculosis.

1840   Dr. Pignier is fired for using books printed in Braille at the National Institute for Blind Youth.

1851   Braille's friends petition the French Government for official recognition of Braille and for the Legion of Honor award for its inventor. This is refused.

1852   Louis Braille dies (January 6). Six months later, the National Institute for Blind Youth adopts Braille as the official reading and writing system.

1860   Braille is tested in schools for the blind in St. Louis, Missouri, and its use spreads to other states.

1868   Dr. Thomas Armitage establishes the English Braille Printing and Publishing House in London.

1952   Braille's body is taken from Coupvray and placed among France's heroes, in the Panthéon in Paris.

Glossary

Antibiotic   A powerful drug that kills harmful germs.
Antiseptic   Free from germs.
By ear   To play musical instruments without the use of written notes, or score.
Cumbersome   Awkward and heavy.
Embossed   Raised from a surface. Embossed letters are raised above the surface of the paper.
Herbal medicine   Medicines made from wild plants said to have special healing powers.
"Night Writing"   A system invented by Captain Charles Barbier, enabling troops to read and transmit messages silently on the battlefield.
Oral teaching   Teaching by spoken word and not from text books.
Organ stops   Knobs or levers used in playing an organ.
Partially-sighted   Not being able to see normally.
Stylus   A pointed instrument used for engraving, drawing or writing.
Tuberculosis   A serious infectious disease of the lungs that was very common during the 19th and early 20th centuries.
Unglazed   Without glass. Unglazed window openings have no glass in them.
Visual memory   The ability to remember the appearance of things that can no longer be seen.

Books to Read

Hall, Candace C. *Shelley's Day: The Day of a Legally Blind Child.* Hartford, CT: Andrew Mountain Press, 1980.
Hunter, Edith. *Child of the Silent Night.* New York: Dell, 1983.
Hunter, Nigel. *Helen Keller.* New York: Franklin Watts/Bookwright, 1985.
Marcus, Rebecca. *Being Blind.* New York: Hastings House, 1981.
Sullivan, Tom and Derek Gill. *If You Could See What I Hear.* New York: New American Library, 1976.

Picture credits

Bruce Coleman (Fritz Prenzel) 29; Mary Evans title page, 15 (upper and lower), 17; Ann Ronan 6, 17, 19, 20, 26; Topham Picture Library 28; Wayland Picture Library 8, 11, 23, 25. Diagram on page 19 by Malcolm Walker.

Index